# In September They Draw Down the Lake

### Suzanne Simmons

AQP
ALEXANDRIA QUARTERLY PRESS
Audubon, New Jersey

Cover image from: "Before the Fall" by Corina Willette
Copyright © Corina Willette

In September They Draw Down the Lake
Copyright © 2020 Suzanne Simmons

Table of Contents

ONE

Sublimation
Commute
After Eating Pizza at Your Grave
Self Portrait as My Mother's Glass Eye
The 10 Cent Tour
No One Needed to Tell Her
I Loved You Early and Deep
Kayak and Loon
Long Overdue

TWO

Boy
In August
Nursery Rhyme
Theory of Mind
A Few Things I Forgot to Ask
Coded
Evening News, Interrupted

THREE

Field Notes
Disbursements
In September They Draw Down the Lake
Stethoscope
Long Night
Lake Effect

# An Introduction by Ilya Kaminsky

I opened this book on *Long Overdue* and was reminded of Charles Simic's claim that the secret wish of all poetry is to stop time. Indeed, I'm stunned by Suzanne Simmons' marvelous ability to do just that: stop time and show us what is on the other side, when all the circumstance is dropped and we are together, in the same room, human to human. She allows us such a human dwelling in 15-16 lines that frankly belong to neither 20th nor 21st century.

### Long Overdue

Early this morning
the phone rang six times
and I followed the bells
out of the dank school hallways
I had been dreaming to the phone.
I pressed it to my ear
and a computerized voice, female,
spoke the words *I'm sorry*.
Then the line went dead.

I considered the many wrongs
in my life, the coddled slights
and old grievances, canyon-deep.
I watched a goldfinch at my feeder,
the muted fall of snow, stretched,
scratched my belly, and said to no one,
*Me, too.*

So *what* is her time? It's a space of a lyric moment. In these lyrics, you will find much humanity, much tenderness, much attentiveness to the details of life here on earth: human to human.

When Simmons shares knowledge with us, she does it through the senses: touch, smell, the vividness of images. She is high minded, yes, but not pretentious. In fact, she is quite the opposite: I was struck by the joyful play in what might, after all, be a sad poem: *Self Portrait as My Mother's Glass Eye*. I was moved, too, by the masterful rhythms in the elegiac clarity of a poem such as *A Few Things I Forgot to Ask:* re-reading it, I am again struck by how in this poem innocence becomes a kind of experience, the asking is the telling. But most of all I keep being stunned by what happens to time in this book, how "The train streaking beside us / blows its whistle, years ago". How does she do it? Perhaps she does it because she knows, intimately, that place is also a time, and memory is also imagination, and imagination is nothing without a heart: "Between my boots and the rutted earth, / a skin of ice breaks." In a time of so much crisis, what a pleasure to read this kind, loving, beautiful work.

Ilya Kaminsky

*For Addie and Rory*

ONE

**Sublimation**

If she slices tomatoes,
feels the skin resist, split,
if she slices tomatoes and the yellow seeds spill,
if she cuts until a wash of juice spreads across
the countertop glazing her fingers coral,
if she keeps the knife steady she will slice only tomatoes:
skin wet petals
seeds like eyes
every door sealed
while outside there's a rumble
like trains under ice

*if the knife should slip*
*if a lid of sky falls*

## Commute

The train is half full,
two seats per rider.
Does that explain this hush?
We are all going to the same place.
It is called Haverhill or Exeter or Durham.
We slide away from bridges and warehouses
into thawing woods. Grey limbs,
a faded sky. No one speaks.
The train is rocking and chanting---
*newhampshire newhampshire newhampshire*
We lean our heads on the cold windows.
Snow is sinking into the earth,
brim and slush, exposure.
One among us can't bear it.
He enters the hinged capsule between cars,
and speaks into his phone.
We watch his lips plead "Hello?"
*newhampshire newhampshire newhampshire---*
The conductor is passing.
He says, Dover, follow me. Dover!
His voice is firm.
Some rise and follow.
Outside, spaces between things
darken to ash.
A yellow moon ascends.
For a time, an abandoned track
runs parallel to ours.
The train streaking beside us
blows its whistle, years ago.
We are almost there.

**After Eating Pizza at Your Grave**

The nasturgeons are in bloom and I miss you,
though our past was faux and we got everything
bass awkward, Mom. Sometimes you threw me
a loop and I flew it—why, just this morning
I bent in the shower and scrubbed the hollow
of my ankle with my thumb, made a shallow pink
bowl of it. You taught me this, When I Became
A Woman, how the dirt sticks there like a bruise.
I wash and wash, and when I borrow a hook or
a coin or a chopping block, I return them promptly.
No one has to ask. You were floundering when you
told me that salmon is the Prozac of the sea,
but it was years before I met a grizzly whose life was
changed by that. Of your eyes, the glass one
had clearer vision. If you could only see
the dolphiniums threading the whitecaps today,
you would know that I mean what I say.

## Self Portrait as My Mother's Glass Eye

I
fell
out
of
you
and
rolled

# The 10 Cent Tour

Here's the boulder
split by a hemlock tree,
a school bus circling the lake
and butterflies spiraling up and up—
sky blue, lake blue—which blue is truest?
Do you know color theory?
Blended complements annihilate each other.
This is my collection of shale
and this is my collection of cellar holes.
You may have one, but not one of each.
Here is the man who molds chocolate bars
on top of his wife; she has clay on her hands,
would you like a taste?
These are the places I am no longer allowed:
butcher shop, bandstand, left field.
But you go ahead—please!
These are the pages of the book I've ironed
and the ones I haven't, yet.

## No One Needed to Tell Her

Everywhere she looked, other
trees, other apples. The snake
was glib but not compelling.
She knew she was naked
by the way the grass clung to her
feet, by the wash of sun behind
her eyelids, the branches abrading
her skin. Everything penetrated.
The apple waited, collected a crescent
of light on one curve, hid its deepest
hues in a pocket of leaves. The branch
fought back when she twisted the stem.
Then, the weight in her palm.
Because she was naked
she arched her neck,
bared her teeth,
punctured the fragrant skin,
the dividing line.
Of course she turned to the other,
offered the fruit, whispered *Love,*

*we are naked,*

*falling.*

*Come.*

## I Loved You Early and Green

I loved you dusky. I loved you low.
Lake, moss, bark, lichen—I touched you
like my own skin. How could I be alone?
Tell me, sweetheart, was I ever in season,
thick with blossom and sap?
In the green wedge of summer
you did your job, setting fires
under my ribs.

(I don't miss you.) I miss air. (I don't miss you.)

**Kayak and Loon**

Suppose we cross the lake together in half-moon light. We'll be black shapes floating between water and sky, between darkness and its shadow. Suppose when you cry my chest vibrates with the sound; this is why I'm here, loon, because I cannot wail as you do with your throat open and full of night. Suppose your cry is a tunnel that carries us so far back in time, the houses on the shore dissolve. All of the cellar holes brim. When you call the horned owl answers, a gurgling screech that ends in a wheeze, and one by one the stars fall down. You wail again, loon, and we drift through the notes and their absence. Stay with me as I dabble in black water,

>  swallow stones to grind
>  in my gut, liquefy my bones,
>  become echo.

## Long Overdue

Early this morning
the phone rang six times
and I followed the bells
out of the dank school hallways
I had been dreaming, to the phone.
I pressed it to my ear
and a computerized voice, female,
spoke the words *I'm sorry.*
Then the line went dead.
I considered the many wrongs
in my life, the coddled slights
and old grievances, canyon-deep.
I watched a goldfinch at my feeder,
the muted fall of snow, stretched,
scratched my belly, and said to no one,
*Me, too.*

TWO

**Boy**

Double knots on your shoes,
a note pinned to your sweater.
On your mat at quiet time you eyed
the jolly felt family. The music lady
sang about silver nutmeg, pursed
her lips and blew into the flute:
notes like spinning globes.
Outside the milkweed pods split
and spit their seeds. No use crying.
The crossing guard had turned his back.
You followed the crows as they pecked
all the crumbs from the trail.

**In August**

I found the boy at the bottom of the lake.
He was wearing yellow shorts.
The ducks' feet swayed like poppies above us.
He took my hand as we walked
through stones circled in silt.
I tried to climb the water but the boy cried out.
Ran my hand through tendrils
swaying and thick. Weightless hand,
weightless head. The lake screams
when it freezes, but a child doesn't know this.
Or that thawing is worse. The thickened cracks,
thins, pulls apart. Clouds of ice drowning,
then blank sky.

## Nursery Rhyme

*Normal healthy baby*
At two he thought he was a machine,
pressed buttons on his tummy:
Fast forward. Rewind.
Can't sing that song.
Bad tape. Holes.

*Ten fingers, ten toes*
At three he counted to a thousand.
Pacing and chanting. Hit the wall, spin,
six hundred and eight. Slam.
Spin. Six hundred and nine.

*First smile, first tooth*
New studies show a problem
with grey matter outstripping the white.
Or, does the white outstrip the grey?
No matter. It looks like this:
10 fingers 10 toes and skin
so thin it is useless. Sounds and smells
ricochet through his body, nerves sizzle
and crack, even the jangle of dark curls is electric.

*Little Bird, Little Bird*
At four the schools began saying no.
Birthday parties and play dates were over.
Experts assembled, mumbling their rosaries.
A-Dee Dee. O-Cee Dee.
P-Dee Dee. P-Dee Dee Enn O Ess.
Asperger's. Autism.

*Normal healthy baby*
At six he asked Mommy, please kill me.
Smeared feces on the dinosaur wallpaper.
Came at me with teeth and eyes wild, clawing.

*Rocking, rocking, rocking*

**Theory of Mind**

*This is Sally. Sally has a basket.*
*This is Anne. Anne has a box.*
*Sally has a marble. She puts the marble in her basket.*
*Sally goes out for a walk.*
*Anne takes the marble out of the basket and puts it in her box.*
*Now Sally comes back.*
*Where will Sally look for her marble?*

                    ---Text from the Sally-Ann Test

I.

Where is the marble?

Look at me. Look at me. Your eyes. Mine.
It's like touching with eyes. Touch the pillow. Paisley.
      I know it hurts.
Touch the marble, it is cold in the way of something
once liquid and hot that cooled, it contains cold
the way a green leaf, having been a bud, could not contain it,
the way salt, left behind by water, contains only dry.
      I know it hurts.
There is no marble. No basket no box. Look at me.
There is no Sally, there is no Anne. No norm. Look at me.
There is no me. There is no you.
      I know it hurts.

II.

Sally will look for her marble
in the eyes of strangers on buses,
under the olive at the bottom of her martini,
in her sock drawer, in the pocket
of her dead father's hunting jacket,
she will look in long vowel sounds,
in the principal's office, she will look
in cerulean, chartreuse and viridian,
Sally will ransack her old friend Anne's house,
she'll fuck Anne's husband and steal
her blue ribbons for good measure,
Sally will file complaints against her neighbors,
she'll become bitter and cheap but she will never stop
looking for her marble, it was *here*, right *here*
in her basket. Sally is nothing if not determined
and we all wish Sally the very best of luck.

## A Few Things I Forgot to Ask

Until recently I only spoke to the living,
people in classrooms, kitchens and barns,
and the ones who handed me coffee through windows.
I yammered away at my children
until the backdoor softly shut.
I opened it to no one there.
So I walked in the woods and tried
to speak with the birds. *No one cooks for me, owl.*
*Peter-peter-whit-FEEbee* the Mockingbird riffed
while the Towhee scolded *Drink your tea!*
but I couldn't master an up-slurred *wheee*,
so I turned uneasily from them,
and spoke to my dead,
those who left me to remember
their crooked spines and straight white teeth
& I wish could ask the name of the cousin
kicked into an early grave by a mule,
how to make jelly from apples and quince,
tart, amber-rose, a soluble jewel,
how to stay married, how to die young
how to un-tongue the syllables
from where they're strung.

**Coded**

I'm sitting on a child-sized chair.
A young woman, a teacher, says
"Something is up."
I look at my husband; he's nodding.
In the noisy room next door
our son orbits his classmates.
Later, we drive home, but we never get there.
The trees have flipped, roots scratch the sky.
All of our neighbors have joined a cult.
Our house has turned on its side.
We adjust. I re-arrange the furniture.
My husband begins crawling for the door.
Seventeen years pass.
I'm sitting on a child-sized chair.
I'm about to speak.

## Evening News, Interrupted

Shots of helicopters, blue lights,
people running with their hands in the air.
*Stay with us for the latest developments!*
—as if the victims might rise and decline the bullets.

Interview with a man who has won the lottery eight times:
*You have to have a strategy.*

In other news/


Outside, the stars are like, like, like…

Most men remind me strongly of my autistic son.
Before him, Christopher Plummer.
Christopher is my strategy.

Turra lurra, hush-a-bye, wondrous way, and why, oh why?
We were going to live in that red farmhouse forever.
The house is still there, and red.

# THREE

**Field Notes**

Things that are silent:
ring fingers, eggshells,
shoes with no feet in them,
looking away, lost wax.
Leftovers again.

Things that are middle:
the difficult child, the years
between childbirth and divorce,
and the middle ear,
which is reasonably efficient
as physical systems go.

Things that may not be silent:
Phosphorous. Mica.
The long journey down
the fallopian tube.

Things that are reasonable:
my husband said that I was not.
He used his stethoscope to keep reason
trotting at his heels.
Be reasonable! Calm down!
But I kept hacking away the dining room table.

**Disbursements**

You take the granite shoulder revealed
when the lake is drawn down.
I'll take the bluets stippling the moss
beneath the birch grove.
You get the sigh of the white dog circling
down to slumber, and the flat stones
taught to pock, pock, pock
the shimmering surface. The jays carving
the dawn into strips of day are mine,
hell, why not throw in the crows?
You were awarded the red canoe,
but that was mine, you know,
all of that drifting, under Orion
and Cassiopeia, fingers trailing,
loon cry, no wake.

## In September They Draw Down the Lake

It was sweet when you held me up,
sweeter still when I dove to your bottom.
Thanks for lapping and churning
and the mornings when you lay under the mist
silent. I was furious every winter when you froze.
Buck up, I thought, fight back a little,
or do you like a lid of ice to hold you down?
Men in trucks drove all over you,
staking claims, drilling holes
and pulling things from you endlessly:
bass, trout, hubcaps, drowned women---
Throw them back!
Oh Lake, you disappoint me so.
The way you wrapped yourself around me felt sincere.
Voices skipped over your surface and I heard every word,
ropes of conversations pulled from cottages and campfires.
Lies, lies, God damn you, Lake.
Nights I floated, seduced, sipping
from your bowl of planets and stars,
but I'll purge myself of you.
Drop by drop I'll drop you,
drop by drop un-drown.

**Long Night**

Cold stuns the lake
into glass. Portal moon.
I've seen other forms:
a skittish path across
the black surface,
flecks of night water
leaping into light.
There is a Hunger Moon,
and one called Crust.

This is the Moon of the Unfuckable.
Between my boots and the rutted earth,
a skin of ice breaks.

**Stethoscope**

He dropped it on the bedside table, the bell aimed at the moon,
a tool for discerning murmurs in the heart, disruptions

in the flow of platelets. She pretended to sleep.
In love he once placed the slim disc to her breast,

diagnosed turbulence in the dark chambers, flamenco.
Years later he tucked their daughter's braids behind her ears,

bent to hear the wheeze in her breath after cartwheel, round-off,
back-walkover. By the glow of a Snoopy nightlight, he caught

the crackle of pneumonia in their son's lungs, a sound
like pulling woolen blankets apart, darting sparks.

Still, she left him. He was on the phone, saying healthy spinal fluid
looks like rainwater. Does it have a sound? Does leaving?

She strained to hear the decades peeling away, car doors slamming,
barred owls courting in the woods, spin cycle, bat crack,

whimper of the dreaming dog, baby cries, come cries,
green wood burning and the hiss of slowly evaporating sap.

## Lake Effect

Two nights before we married
I was awake until dawn, listening
to the insistent lapping of the lake.
I was restless. I wanted the water still.
And the wedding night—do you remember?
Hard rain and thunder while we made
our bed in a pocket of candlelight,
hushed, exhausted, in the honeymoon cabin?
This was your lake then, your gift to give,
godlike. Days and nights our bodies slid through it,
stitched the elements with our limbs.

This autumn I rent a house
with a northern exposure,
the shoreline deeply shadowed.
Between us lies the untamed island
we circled in our canoe, a dense tangle of pine,
beech and granite, voiced by loons,
their crazed cackles and yips of alarm,
and the shivery tunnels of their mournful cries,
cries that call across time
to a world before humans.

They cut through my dreams. Wake me.
Do you hear them? You on your shore?

Acknowledgements

Alexandria Quarterly: "In August"
Calyx: A Journal of Art and Literature by Women: "Long Night"
Fifth Wednesday: "Disbursements"
Talisman: A Journal of Contemporary Poetry and Poetics: "Evening News, Interrupted," and "Field Notes"
burntdistrict: "After Eating Pizza at Your Grave"
Miramar: "Commute"

Under the title Limnology this chapbook was a finalist for the Bright Hill Chapbook Competition and a semifinalist for the Claudia Emerson Poetry Chapbook Award and the Concrete Wolfe Chapbook Competition

With gratitude to the women whose friendship sustains me: Markie Babbott, poetry road-buddy, provider of metaphors, titles, and occasional therapy—I bless the day we met! Laura Simmons, my sister and oldest friend, thank you always. I'm grateful to my far-flung pod: Corina Willette, Barbara Bradley-Rutz and Valerie Shurer-Christle—long may we roam. Thank you Lael Robertson, Holly Hurd, Samantha Storey, Kristen Biers-Jones, and Lynn Perrin-Wilhousky. Thank you to my incredible writing group: Janet Chwalibog, Suzanne Mosley, Joanne Powers and Gail Spector. Thanks to Doug and Renn Simmons and Pam Strong. Harley Heath, thank you for then. To my many poetry teachers, especially my MFA mentors Katie Farris, Carol Frost, Ilya Kaminsky and Malena Morning, my deepest gratitude.

Suzanne Simmons' poems, essays and photographs have been published in the NYTimes, Fifth Wednesday, Rattle, Smartish Pace, The Baltimore Review and numerous other journals. She lives in Eliot, ME.

Made in the USA
Middletown, DE
13 January 2021